ISBN: 9781314440881

Published by:
HardPress Publishing
8345 NW 66TH ST #2561
MIAMI FL 33166-2626

Email: info@hardpress.net
Web: http://www.hardpress.net

Mrs. Plummer Harris.

THE SHADOW BETWEEN HIS SHOULDER-BLADES

Other Books by Joel Chandler Harris

Uncle Remus—His Songs and His Sayings
Nights with Uncle Remus
Uncle Remus and His Friends
Mingo
Little Mr. Thimblefinger
On the Plantation
Daddy Jake, the Runaway
Balaam and His Master
Mr. Rabbit at Home
The Story of Aaron
Sister Jane
Free Joe
Stories of Georgia
Aaron in the Wild Woods
Tales of the Home Folks
Georgia, from the Invasion of De Soto to Recent Times
Evening Tales
Stories of Home Folks
Chronicles of Aunt Minerva Ann
On the Wing of Occasions
The Making of a Statesman
Gabriel Tolliver
Wally Wanderoon
A Little Union Scout
The Tar Baby Story and Other Rhymes of Uncle Remus
Told by Uncle Remus
The Bishop and the Boogerman

An' how could he, of all men, be so cold an' so cruel?"

See page

THE SHADOW BETWEEN HIS SHOULDER-BLADES

BY

JOEL CHANDLER HARRIS

WITH ILLUSTRATIONS
BY
GEORGE HARDING

BOSTON
SMALL, MAYNARD AND COMPANY
PUBLISHERS

THE UNIVERSITY PRESS, CAMBRIDGE, U. S. A.

ILLUSTRATIONS

"An' how could he, of all men, be so cold an' so cruel?" . . . . *Frontispiece*

"At one house along the way we swapped the rumor for a drink of water" . . . . . *Page* 36

"'What are you doin' here?' he says to ol' Drew, lookin' like he was gwine to bite his head off" . . . . „ 66

"'Stan' back from the door, whoever you are!'" . . . . „ 128

THE SHADOW BETWEEN HIS SHOULDER-BLADES

THE SHADOW BETWEEN HIS SHOULDER-BLADES

I

He rode for to ease his conscience, he rode for to rest his soul;
He followed the flying heron where the Western clouds unroll,
Till war spread out before him its black and smoking scroll.
— *Herndon's Ballad of the Outrider.*

ONE of the pleasing features of Shady Dale was its wide streets. As Mr. Billy Sanders said, everybody had a chance to turn around twice without knocking the other fellow down. The wide streets were a part of the plans of Raleigh Clopton, the first settler, and they gave to the town a beauty and a charm that still survive. The streets being wide, the courthouse square must needs be spacious, and the restful perspective it offers to the eye is hardly duplicated in any other town.

The tavern faces the square, and its wide and inviting veranda is, perhaps, the most popular resort in the entire neighborhood, especially in warm weather. For a long time Mr. Billy Sanders has made it his headquarters, and this fact, no doubt, has added to its popularity. A visitor to the town was sitting on this veranda one day, listening to the entertaining conversation of Mr. Sanders, when a tall man, with gray hair, rode across the square and disappeared down one of the wide avenues that lead away from the center of the town. Mounted as he was on a fine gray horse, and swaying to its motions as if he were a part of the creature, he presented a very picturesque figure to the eye of the stranger, who made haste to say as much.

"Thar ain't but one Wimberly Driscoll," Mr. Sanders replied, "an' that 's him. It 's a livin' wonder that his restlessness ain't eat him up or burnt him out long ago. He 's got a plantation out here a mile or two, an' he runs it like it was a dry-goods store. They tell a tale about one er his great uncles that 'll give you a better idee of Wimberly Driscoll than I can. They say he was a black-haired, gray-eyed man, jest like Wimberly. He was a missionary Baptist, an' he took his Bible an' a big walkin'-stick an' went out arter the heathen. They wanted to make hash of him when they fust seed him, but he jest backed up ag'in' a mud-shanty an' preached 'em a good strong sermon wi' his walkin'-cane. The Lord must 'a' been right wi' 'im, bekaze when he had whipped 'em out, an' got 'em kinder 'umble, he took 'em by the scruff of their necks an' soused 'em in a mud-puddle; an' then, wi' a stick in one hand and the Bible in the other, he made 'em kneel in pra'r an' give thanks for the'r conversion."

The visitor laughed at this method of converting the heathen, but Mr. Sanders pretended to be very solemn.

"That 's Wimberly all over," he went on; "he runs his farm wi' a club an' the multiplication table, an' you can't git his han's away from 'im for love nor money. He 's got ever'thing screwed up so tight that ef a spring was to break the whole county 'd be kivvered wi' meat an' wheat an' lint cotton. A railroad agent come through here two or three year ago, an' tried to hire some of his han's to go to Massysip. The fust one he ax'd settled the whole business. 'Who? Me! No, suh! I don't want Mr. Driscoll ter be ridin' dat fur des fer me!' You 'd think from that that they was all afear'd of him; but that ain't the feelin' they 've got. You look like you mought be from Chicago? Oh, Ohio! Well, that lets you clean out, bekaze ef you hain't been a-livin' here all your life, I 'll never be able for to tell you what I mean. All I can say is that Wimberly is Wimberly, an' ef he 'd 'a' been any Wimblier I dunno what would 'a' happened. Ef anybody knows him, I reckon I oughter be the one, bekaze I made a little campaign wi' 'im that kinder turned my stomach ag'in' war."

"It must have been interesting," the stranger said.

"You could make your language twicet as hot," replied Mr. Sanders, "an' still it would n't be nigh warm enough. As long as me an' Wimberly Driscoll stay on top of the groun' you kin jest tell ever'-body you meet that all the fools ain't dead yit. Fust an' fo'most, me an' him was put out of business about the same time, ef not the same day. He lost his right foot in Verginny, whilst he was caperin' about on the breastworks, an' I got plugged in the gizzard at the battle of Chickamauga. I felt like some un had hit me wi' a red-hot stove, an' then I dreamed that I had been curled up on account of a peck of green apples I eat when I was a boy. The green apple idee put me in mind of home, an' set me to honin' an' pinin' for the faces an' places I use to know. The doctors whetted the'r knives on the soles of the'r boots an' got the ball out'n my entra'ls. One on 'em was a ol' friend of mine, Doc. Dorrin'ton, an' he hustled about an' got me a furlough, an' home I come.

"I reckon the sight of home must 'a' been too much for my tender heart, bekaze I had n't been here long before I keeled over an' went to bed good an' hard, wi' nothin' for to do but count the nail-holes in the ceiling, an' listen to the dogwood-bark tea a-zoonin' in my y'ears like a dozen ripe lady muskeeters a-cryin' for the'r true loves. Doc. Dorrin'ton got word of this at the front, an' stedder addin' a month or more to my furlough, he sent me a discharge. From the way it read, you 'd 'a' thought that the whole Confederacy had come to the conclusion to secede from William H. Sanders, late of said Southern States. I took the blow as easy as I could; I said that ef Mr. Davis an' Giner'l Bragg could stan' it I could. I mought 'a' cried a little, but I took mighty good keer not to do it in public. It was what the gals an' boys that do our noveling call a secret grief, like a pot that biles over while the cook is out in the yard talkin' to your neighbor's gyard'ner.

"I got use to it arter a while, an', when I did, I got well, an' I hain't had a day's sickness from that time tell right now — an' ef I ain't much mistaken, it 's mighty nigh half arter ten, in the year Eighteen Hunderd-an'-Close-at-Home."

The stranger looked at Mr. Sanders curiously, but nothing but good humor shone in his blue eyes and beaming face.

"It don't take a discharged soldier long for to git well when he knows that the conscript officer can't lay hands on him, an' when they tol' me that Wimberly Driscoll was at home, sufferin' from the corns on the foot he left in Virginia, I went right off for to see ef I could n't help him out.

"An' thar he was, frettin' like a colt wi' his head tied to a tree. I dunno ef you could call it a happy family, wi' ol' Mammy Kitty churnin' like she was mad, an' sloshin' the clabber out on the floor, an' ol' Jimmy Myrick a-takin' snuff an' sneezin', while his little fice dog scratched for fleas, hittin' his hocks on the floor like thar was somebody knockin' at the door in a hurry for to git in. I took in the whole business before ol' Jimmy could shuffle 'roun' an' git me a cheer, an' I laid off for to give Wimberly the best I had in my shop. I told him tales, an' jollied him wi' a mighty free han', an' in a little or no time some color show'd in his face, an' his gray eyes begun for to sparkle. You know how these dark-complected people do: when they git by themselves they drop down into the depths, an' they ain't no depth too deep for 'em. He forgot all about his foot in Virginia, an' he laughed so loud that ol' Jimmy Myrick could n't set an' sleep in any comfort. He was constantly mumblin' to hisself, an' takin' snuff an' sneezin'. When I went to go Mammy Kitty holler'd at me: 'Don't stay 'way long, Marse Billy! Dat boy done laugh mo' dis day dan he laugh sence de war!'

"But Wimberly Driscoll got more restless ever' day that passed. He was head over heels in love wi' the Featherston gal — Margaret Featherston was her name — an' it looked like that this love had kinder struck in sorter like the measles when you ketch cold. It 's a mighty good thing that it 's a disease that ain't ketchin', bekaze I reckon I 'd 'a' been gallopin' roun' the neighborhood on my all-fours an' barkin' at the moon. I tried redicule on him, but I jest mought as well 'a' flung warm bread at a hongry dog; an' the upshot of it was that he took a notion that

he oughter hunt for service under Gener'l Forrest. I ast him for to let me go
in his place, seein' as how I was a sound
man. But that jest riled him. He said
he 'd be glad ef I went wi' 'im, but he
would n't hang 'roun' here doin' nothin',
not ef he was to git shot by the time he
got out'n the yard.

"Well, we figger'd the matter out. He
had a fine gray mar', an' I had the rackin'
roan. Both on 'em had been hid out from
the Government pressin' agent, an' thar
wa'n't no better specimens of horse-flesh
in the whole of our beloved Confederacy
— an' that ain't no joke! A gal in a ham-
mock would n't have no easier time than
the right party on the rackin' roan, an'
the gray mar' was jest as good. You
may think it mighty funny, but, when a
man 's been to war, somethin' nice goes
out'n him; he ain't the same; he gits

oneasy, an' the Ol' Boy creeps up an' grips him in the neighborhood of his thinkin' machine. It 's took me these many long years for to git rid of the feelin'.

"Wimberly had more trouble than I did when the time come to start. He had to deal wi' ol' Mammy Kitty, an' ef she did n't give him a dressin' down I 'll never take another chaw of terbacker! He had n't more 'n got on the gray mar' before ol' Kitty opened up, an' she preached his funer'l, an' she preached it at the top of her voice. Ef one of you Northern fellers could 'a' heern 'er, you 'd 'a' got a bran' new idee in regards to the oppressed colored people. She told him he looked mighty much like fightin' somebody. 'Don't wave yo' han' at me!' she squalled. 'Give yo' good-bys ter dem what want um. I know what you gwine atter; you ain't huntin' no fightin'! No! not you! You er huntin' dat gal which her mammy took an' tooken'd away fum here! I hope you 'll fin' her, an' I hope she 'll kick you higher dan de sky!'"

The stranger marveled at the ease with which Mr. Sanders brushed his own personality aside, and became, for a moment apparently, an old negro woman whose grief made her wild and vicious.

"She holler'd all this at the top of her voice, an' she kep' it up ontell she broke down an' boo-hooed. Then she started in ag'in, an' as fur as we could hear 'er, she was belittlin' an' abusin' the boy she had raised. It was all she could do, and she done like she had served her time at the trade. Driscoll has got the wust temper you ever saw in a white man, but he jest rode along an' paid no attention to

Mammy Kitty, except to laugh when she said somethin' he know'd was the truth. 'I reckon, Mr. Sanders,' says he, 'that she 's e'en about the only livin' human bein' in this worl' that really loves me. You know,' he says, 'the kinder love that makes anybody mad wi' you one minnit, an' cry for you the next, is the only sort that 's wuth havin'.' I declar' to gracious, I was right sorry for the youngster, but I never let him know it. I jest give the roan a quarter of an inch more rein, an' we ambled down the big road, with a feelin' that we had the world an' a big part of the woods be-'fore us.

"But it wa'n't no purty figger that we cut. Wimberly had a crutch strapped 'longside his saddle; his uniform that had been so fine had faded so it had to be home-dyed — an' you know what that means. It was in two fast colors an' one that 'd run. I had on a bran new suit er brown jeans, an' it belied me by makin' a country farmer out'n me. Arter the fust half-hour we took our time, an' let the creeturs foller the'r own notions. I was ridin' 'long lookin' at the roan's front feet, when, all of a sudden, Driscoll whirled in an' begun to swear like a trooper. 'Ef I had that ol' nigger 'oman here,' says he, 'I 'd give her the wust frailin' that the ol' dickens ever got!' Wi' that he p'inted up the road, an' thar stood his fav'rite houn'. 'I made ol' Peter fasten that dog in the barn,' says he, 'an' now yonder he is! Ol' Mammy Kitty has turned him aloose jest for spite. Confound her old hide!'

"Sure enough, thar stood the dog. He did n't look gay, an' he did n't look glad. It looked like he had jest come out in the road a hunderd or two yards ahead for to see how Wimberly would take it. His tail was hangin' down, an' appariently he was lookin' for a whippin'. Wimberly called 'im, but the tone of his voice did n't suit the dog; it looked like he know'd that, ef he come to the call, he 'd be driv' back, an' so he jest turned into the woods ag'in an' bided his time. You nee'n' to tell me that a dog can't think, bekaze they kin; an' that houn' know'd jest as well as his master did that, ef he come when he was called, he 'd git the word to go back, an' that was why he went away ahead before he showed hisself. Well, narry one on us could do anything but go on, an' go on we did.

"Thar 's no call for you to believe it, but when we had got too fur for the dog to be driv' back, he j'ined the cavalry-cade, lookin' mighty sheepish. Wimberly abused him as well as he could, but the dog know'd by the tone of his voice that he did n't mean it, an' wi' that he jumped up, kissed the gray mar' on the end of her nose, an' went sailin' up the road an' into the woods. He had n't been gone long before we heern 'im tree a squirrel. Wimberly looked at me and laughed jest like a sixteen-year-old boy. We paid no attention to the dog, bekaze we could n't lose him, not onless the cree-turs we was ridin' took wings an' left the ground; all he had to do was to come back to the road, pick up the trail, an' make free wi' his knowledge; an' that 's jest what he done. When he found out that we wa'n't on no huntin' expedi-tion, he jest sobered up, an' trotted along at the gray mar's heels as tame as one of these chany fices that half-rich folks set in a cold place in the parlor.

"We fetched a snack of vittles along, an' when our shadders was at the'r shortest we stopped at a spring we know'd, an' tol' one another ever'thing we know'd about war an' peace, an' ol' line politics, when State rights was somethin' more than a headline in a weekly paper. An' then, when silence fell, as the poet says, we begun to inquire wharbouts we 'd have our snugglin'-place for the night. Mind you, in camp we 'd been sleepin' on the ground, wi' fence-rails for mattresses, an' the roof of creation for a kivver, an' here we was disputin' at whose door we 'd knock.

"Wimberly was for ridin' straight ahead ontell late bedtime an' trust to luck. I know well that what you call luck is mighty nice when it comes off on time; but I 'd lots ruther put my dependence on Providence an' common-sense. We made up our minds to stop at Lije Vinin's. Both on us know'd him an' his wife. Lije was e'en about my age, we 'd been good frien's for I dunno how many year, an' Wimberly know'd 'im mighty nigh as well. We calcalated, goin' at the gait we was, that we 'd land at Lije's private tavern somewhere in the neighborhood of supper-time, an' we ruther reckoned that we 'd git a good one.

"Well, we come mighty nigh calcalatin' right, the diffunce bein' on the side of night when we thought it 'ud be early candlelight. We must 'a' loiter'd along, tellin' tales an' swappin' jokes. Anyhow, we come to Lije's big gate, it was dark; an' more 'n than that, jest as we rid up the gate flew open an' three men rode out at a gallop, an' before we could git done dodgin' an' ketch our breath, here come another man ridin' a mule, an' it was all we could do to keep him from runnin' over us. It was dark, but not dark enough to shut out ever'thing, an' the rider that come mighty nigh runnin' over us was a nigger, an' he was a-ridin' a-straddle of a mule. I know'd the mule an' I know'd the nigger, but not a word did I say to Driscoll, who had all he could do to look arter the gray mar'. The three men that fust galloped out went the way that we was gwine, but the nigger an' the mule went the way we had jest come.

"I says to Wimberly: 'Did n't the gear of them men's horses rattle like they was soldiers?'

"Wimberly, he says: 'It certainly did, sence you 've mentioned it.'

"We could n't 'a' done anything onless we 'd 'a' know'd they was comin'; we did n't have time for to tell 'em nuther howdy nor good-by. They whiffed past an' was gone. I could 'a' pulled the nigger off'n his mule, but I did n't have time for to make up my mind what to do. We stood thar wonderin' for quite a little spell, an' then we rode in. Somehow or nuther, it seemed to be my time for to knock at the door. I done it as perlitely as I could. Nobody did n't come, an', arter so long a time, I knocked ag'in, hittin' a louder whack, but still genteel. Presently, a nigger boy come slippin' aroun' the house from the back way. He was so skeer'd that he could n't say a word, an' he stood thar gaspin' an' chokin' ontell I grabbed him by the collar an' yerked him aroun' a time or two.

"'Whadder you mean, you lim' of Satan?' says I. 'An' why n't you spit out what you 've got on your min', ef you 've got a min'?'

"The shakin' kinder fetched 'im to, an' he stuttered out that his mistiss had sent him aroun' the house for to see ef we was Yankees, an', ef we was, to tell us to pack up an' leave.

"'Yankees!' says I. 'Why, they ain't one on 'em nigher than a little ways this side of Chattanooga.'

"The nigger swelled up like he was gwine to bust: 'Ya-ya-yasser, dey is, kaze th'ee un um done took supper here, an' des now galloped off! I seed um wid my own eyeballs!' Then he told us that, ef we was anybody his mistiss know'd, we was to come aroun' the back way, bekaze she would n't open the front door for the Queen of England.

"Well, to the back we went, an' Mary Ann Vinin', the cook and the house gal was all huddled up in the kitchen mighty nigh skeer'd to death. They looked jest like thar had been a earthquake, an' they was lookin' for to be swaller'd up ever' minit.

"'Mary Ann,' says I, 'what in the world is the matter?'

"I 'd been a-knowin' Mary Ann Vinin' a mighty long time, an' when she hearn my voice, an' come out whar she could see me, she jest fetched one squall: 'Oh, Mr. Sanders!' — an' fell over like she 'd been blow'd down by a gust of wind. She wa'n't one of the faintin' kind, but she sighed herself to sleep that time. An' then, when she come to, an' had kinder ketched her breath a time or two, she was as mad as Tucker. Me an' Wimberly Driscoll did n't nigh believe that thar had been any Yankees aroun', an' this made her madder. You know when a 'oman reely gits mad she 's wuss 'n a shuck brier-bush with a hornet's nest in its bosom.

"Mary Ann was so mad that thar wa'n't nothin' too mean for her to say, especially as we was most like home-folks. Fust an' fo'most she believed that we was in cahoots wi' the Yankees that had skeer'd her; she was shore of it, bekaze one on 'em was Bushrod Claiborne, an' we all know'd him. Driscoll blushed an' I laughed, an' Mary Ann got madder. She know'd they was our partners, bekaze one on 'em fetched a note for Wimberly Driscoll, an' ef we did n't know nothin' about the Yankees, how was it that we come in so pat? She'd like to know that an' a heap of other things that looked mighty funny. Wi' that, the house gal up'd an' vowed that the Yankees did n't fetch that note.

"'Who, then?' says Mary Ann.

"'Unc. Peter Driscoll,' says the gal.

"'That's so,' says I, 'bekaze I seed ol'

Peter ride through the gate on a mule, right arter the three men skipped.'

"'You did n't tell me,' says Driscoll, bridlin' up.

"'Why, no,' says I, 'for I was n't quite certain an' shore, but I know now that the man on the mule was ol' Peter, an' nobody else.'

"'We left him at home,' says Wimberly, facin' me out.

"'I can't help that!' says I. 'Ol' Peter rode out right arter the three men, an' come mighty nigh runnin' over me.'

"'Well, where is the note?' says Wimberly. 'Thar must be some trouble at home.'

"'Here it is,' says Mary Ann, 'an' a mighty purty thing it is. Take it, an' le' me go wash my han's!'

"Well, the note was mighty funny lookin'. It had been handled in its journey ontell it was mighty nigh as black as the back of a cultivated fireplace. Wimberly took it an' turned it over in his han' like he was afeard it 'ud blow up an' singe his eyebrows. I can' rickerleck percisely the words, but the note said that, ef Wimberly Driscoll ever give a thought to Margaret Featherston, the time had done come for him to prove it. Then it went on to say that she was mighty close to trouble, an' mighty miser'ble. The note said it was wrote by one that Wimberly never saw, an' that the Featherston gal did n't know it was wrote, but the fact that she was close to trouble ought to be enough for Wimberly Driscoll to know. It ain't nothin' but the truth when I tell you that his face was so red it could 'a' tetched off a keg of powder. The note was a whole sheet of foolscap, folded, an' on a part of it somebody had wrote jest two words: ‘Graylands, Memphis.’ When they read that out, I says, ‘Ef that ain’t in the Union lines you kin shoot me wi’ the fust pop-gun you find in the road.’

“‘That ’s where her cousin lives,’ says Wimberly; ‘that ’s where she went when she left Shady Dale’ — an’ he looked like a man in a dream.

“By that time Mary Ann had kinder cooled off — no ’oman kin keep her dander up long at a time when she gits a whiff of somethin’ that looks like love, e’en ef it ’s no more than the ghost on it. Says Mary Ann, chokin’ her errytation: ‘Don’t you remember, Wimberly, how you an’ Margaret use to spend your Saturday holidays at my house? You know you do! Why, you an’ Margaret use to be mighty fond of one another — don’t deny it!’”

Mr. Sanders threw his head back with a simpering smile that convulsed the stranger and others who had gradually come forward to hear what new yarn the old Georgian was spinning.

"Wimberly did n't deny it, an' Mary Ann made a big flutter over the whole business. He did n't have much to say, an' I ruther got the idee from the way he done that thar had been some kind of a misunderstandin' betwixt um while Wimberly was at college — one of them kind of misunderstandin's that a fly could n't light on. Arter a while we mosied off to bed, bekaze we had to make a soon start the next mornin'. The stutterin' boy called us, an' we had to eat breakfus by candlelight. Soon as it was, Mary Ann was up.

"'Wimberly,' says she, 'I dremp about you last night — you an' Margaret Featherston — an' I did n't see no harm come to you in my dreams. But thar 's one question I want to ast you: Ef them Yankees did n't fetch that note, how did ol' Peter git his han's on it? Now, ef you 'll tell me that, I 'll not pester you no more. Whar in the roun' world did ol' Peter git hold of it?'

"Wimberly shuck his head.

"Says I: 'It 's as easy as a feather-bed. It started wi' a nigger in Tennes-see, an' it passed from han' to han' ontell it come to Peter, an' he, hearin' us say we 'd likely stop at your house, got a mule, cut through by the plantation roads an' beat us.'

"We took to the road — gun, crutch, hosses, an' houn' — not much of a army, but a right smart of a scoutin' party. We took our time, but thar wa'n't no jokin' done. Wimberly Driscoll was broodin' over somethin', an' I wa'n't feelin' peart enough for to laugh ef we 'd a met a funer'l percession. The fust house we come to, the childern was settin' on the fence like they was watchin' for somethin', an' as soon as they seed us they tumbled off like some un had flung a stick at 'em, an' run in the house, hollerin': 'Run, Pap! Run, Ma! The Yankees is comin'!' I know'd by that that somethin' had happened, an' I felt bound for to find out what it was. My folks allers tol' me that cur'osity would be the death of me, an' I reckon it will; but that did n't cut no figger in them days. So I spurred up the rackin' roan, an' rid in for to see what the trouble could be. I went in sech a hurry that I caught sight of the 'oman runnin' to'rds a pine thicket for dear life. It was Betsey Dillard, an' I holler'd at her, callin' her name, an' she stopped, an' come back, lookin' purty hot in the neighborhood of the place whar the dewlap says howdy to the neck.

"'What in the world?' says I.

"'You may well sesso,' says she, 'ef you was in my place an' weighed three hunderd pounds. Why, I've been ready to run for the thicket any minnit sence yistiddy arternoon, when a passel of Yankees come ridin' by, an' made me give 'em some buttermilk.'

"'Yankees?' says I.

"'Yes, indeed,' says she, 'an' a whole passel on 'em at that. They was a part of Wilson's raiders. I dunno what damage they done, an' I thank the Lord that they ain't burnt us out'n house an' home!'

"Now, all that was news to me, but my mind went back to what Mary Ann Vinin' said about Bushrod Claiborne.

"Claiborne was a gentleman hoss-drover, an' he use to come to Shady Dale ever' season. He was some kin to Margaret Featherston — a long way off, I reckon — an' he made use of that fact for to kinder drap his wing at 'er, an' it got so that people said he was dead in love wi' 'er. When it come to that, purty nigh all the boys in the town was in the same fix, includin' Wimberly Driscoll, Esq., an' et cetery. I reckon Bushrod was the fust man that ever got Wimberly's dander up. He bought the mammy of the mar' he was ridin' from Bushrod, an' when he come South the next season he claimed to have a sheer in the foal she 'd dropped. Along about that time Wimberly wa'n't nothin' but a boy nohow, he wa'n't out'n his teens; but when Claiborne made that claim in a crowd, he jest up an' told 'im what he thought on him. He called him ever' name he could think of, an' when Claiborne said somethin' about boys — when he said he did n't fight childern — why, I jest put in an' ast 'im ef he had any objection to mixin' up wi' a man a leetle older than he was. He ain't answered me to this day. He jest growled out somethin' an' slunk off. That was jest before the war fever begun to make the fellers beller for blood, an' I don't believe I laid eyes on Bushrod ontell he come through our town on his way to Richmond, as he said, for to j'ine his fortunes wi' the fortunes of the Confederacy, an' now here he was runnin' wi' the enemy.

" Says I to Wimberly Driscoll: ' Brace up, my son; we 'll have to deal wi' Bushrod Claiborne before we 're done wi' this business.'

"Wimberly looked at me jest like a man wakin' up. Says he: 'What I 'm a-gwine to do is to offer my services to Forrest.'

"'Tooby shore!' says I; 'but all the same, you 've got Memphis wrote on your manly forrerd, an' I dunno but what I 'm in the same fix. I can tell you what the trouble is: the Memphis Featherston is for the Union, an' the Georgia Featherston is for the Confederacy. Olivia Featherston, who come after Margaret and her mammy, is the daughter of the man we used to call the Kentucky Featherston. He was a red an' ripe Clay man, an' had made hisself so prominent in the political lodge that he took the degree of Colonel. Olivia, his daughter, was left by herself when the Colonel died, an' that 's the reason she tolled the Georgia Featherston up thar. She 's twenty-eight year old, an' she 'd be a ol' maid ef she wa'n't so fresh-lookin'.'

"At that, Wimberly begun for to git jealous. Says he:

"'How do you know all that?'

"Says I: 'I have come to the time of life when it 'd be as easy for me to be a ol' 'oman as it is to be a man. Sech bein' the case, why ax me whar I got my information?'"

By this time Mr. Sanders had an audience of at least a dozen people.

"Well," he went on, turning to the stranger, "bimeby we come to whar we could hear gossip about Gener'l Forrest. A ol' man, a 'oman, an' a whole passel of childern passed us on the road. Ever' time we 'd ax a question the 'oman would bust out cryin' an' say that Gener'l Forrest was dead wi' the lockjaw on account of a wound in his foot. An' from that time on the big road an' the by-paths was constantly full of folks tryin' to git to some place whar they could n't smell powder. That was a new side of war to me, an' I never could git used to it. The rumor that Forrest was dead did n't add nothin' to our appetites, but we made the best out'n it we could.

"At one house along the way we swapped the rumor for a drink of water. A young an' good-lookin' 'oman was settin' on the doorstep watchin' the capers of a two-year-old toddler, an' she was so mad when she heern the news that ef she 'd 'a' been a man she 'd 'a' cussed. She made denial of it so quick an' hard that ef I had n't 'a' been on horseback I 'd 'a' dodged. Then she made denial of it ag'in an' bust out cryin'.

"'It ain't so,' says she. 'It 's a lie, I don't keer who tells it! It ain't in natur'

"At one house along the way we swapped the rumor for a drink of water"

that he 's dead — he 's got too much to do, too much to live for.'

"Then a man wi' gray ha'r come to the door of the cabin. Says he:

"'What ye whinin' about, honey? What 's the men said to ye? The Gener'l dead! Shoo! you can't make me believe that ontell I see 'im on his coolin' board. The good Lord ain't gwine to make Bush Claiborne that happy in this world!'

"Says I: 'Then you know Bushrod Claiborne?'

"The old man snapped back at me like a rattlesnake: 'Well, I reckon we know 'im. You see that young un out thar? Well, that 's how much we know 'im!'

"'But, pap,' says the gal, 'he 's comin' back; he said he would; I jest know he is.'

"The ol' feller growled at 'er jest like a dog does when he 's about to bite. Ef ever I seed vengeance in a man's eye I seed it then.

"'Is he? Is he?' he says. 'You reckon he will? Well, jest let him! Jest let him show his filthy face whar I kin see it!'

"I tell you what, we rode away considerably sobered. The gal was cryin' easy like, an' we never said a word to one another for a mighty long time. The whole sorry tale had been laid out as cle'r to our understandin' as a big map of the world wi' blood-red lines printed on it. Never, sence man could make mouths at his neighbor, was a tale kivverin' such grief an' misery told in fewer words. It struck me through an' through, an' I says to myself:

"'The Lord send that Bushrod Claiborne gits his deserts in this world an' the next!'

"As we went the procession of reffagees got longer an' longer. 'T was all mighty pitiful, but somehow or nuther I could n't git Bushrod Claiborne out'n my min', bekaze I little expected for to find a sample of his devil's work in this fur-off country. Yit I reckon that in the eyes of the Almighty the world ain't bigger than a faulty apple, an' ever' bit as wormy.

"Now, while we was ridin' along, chawin' on sech cuds as our minds 'd give up to us, I happened to raise my eyes an' right thar, in full sight, I seed a lot of boys in blue swarmin' across the road ahead of us. They swarmed across like they was preparin' for the smoky business of war, an' presently a light battery of four guns went hoppin' across arter them. The hosses stopped still of the'r own accord, an' the houn', wi' bristles raised, slunk off in the bushes, an' stood thar whinin' like he was afeard. For a long minnit — too long for me — we stood thar, waitin' for to see what was gwineter happen next. I had the feelin' that the whole thing was a part of a show that had been fixed up specially for us.

"Bimeby, the gray mar' got restless, an' she retched out one forefoot an' hit the groun' a whack that sounded like the thing the newspapers call a thud. I never seed one myself nor heern it, but that 's the way it sounded. The whack woke us up an' we took to the woods on our left. The hosses did n't make so much fuss, considerin', an' Wimberly's houn' jumped ahead for all the world like 't was gwine huntin'."

II

Right merrily in the woodland he hid and dodged and fled,
With the enemy following after, and the heron flying ahead,
Over fields forever fallow, over hills forever red.
— The Herndon Ballads.

"WE had no idee whar we was gwine, an' the small timber was so thick that we couldn't see no more than twenty yards ahead. Thar wa'n't no help for it, an' we had to trust to Providence an' the hosses. When we did git out'n the bushes, it seemed like we was out shore enough. A level cle'rin' stretched out in front of us, an' it looked like it got bigger an' bigger in the distance. The bushes an' the underbrush foller'd it as fur as they could, an' skirted the cle'rin' for a mile or more, as much as to say that ef they couldn't go no furder they would n't let the prairie land scrouge 'em clean out'n business.

"The timber skirted the cle'rin' in the shape of the new moon, an' the hosses, left to their own notions, made for the horn that lay to the right. They sorter peartened up in the'r gait, an' Wimberly's houn' run ahead doin' like he smelt the trail of a fox. But, presently, the gray mar' begun for to go slower, an' the roan slacked up. Then they stopped short, jest like they seed or smelt somethin' they 'd never seed before, an' throw'd up the'r heads, an' made the funny kind of a fuss that 's betwixt a snort an' a whinny, like hosses allers does when they 're kinder suspicious of the'r surroundin's. But the houn', he went right ahead like he was runnin' to the music of a fiddle played in jig-time. When he got close to the bushes that made one end of the horn I was tellin' you about, he stopped like some un had spoke to him, lowered his tail, raised his bristles, an' begun for to back to'rds us — bayin' like he had treed forty-'lev'n 'possums. He had a mighty purty mouth, too, an' it sorter sounded like a note on a horn. I reckon you could 'a' heern 'im more 'n a mile. He backed an' bayed, an' when he got whar he thought he could n't be ketched, he turned tail an' run right behind the hosses.

"You don't know much, I reckon, about the old-time Southern saddlers?" said Mr. Sanders, turning to the stranger, who was perhaps the most appreciative listener in the little group gathered around the old Georgian. "Well, they was trained to go all the gaits — for-'erds, back'erds, an' sideways. We did n't want to turn tail an' run, an' so we made the hosses back away. Thar wa'n't nothin' in sight for to back away from, an' yet we know'd p'int-blank that the enemy was some'rs behind the timber. I reckon the barkin' of the houn' fooled 'em, bekaze it ain't once in a long while that you see a man gwine to war wi' a dog amongst his belongin's.

"I kept my eyes purty much to'rds the re'r, bekaze I did n't want the roan to back over a stump or into a gully, an' arter a while my eyes fell on a ravine right behind us. I called Wimberly's attention to it, an' we turned the hosses 'roun' and made for it. By the time we got in speakin' distance of the place we was stopped by a voice that sounded like it was use to shoutin' out orders:

"'B'ar to the right!' it said. 'B'ar to the right, an' be quick about it!'

"It was the voice of a grown man, an' the way he said it satisfied me that we'd better do what we was told to do ef we wanted for to stay in that part of the country wi' any peace of mind. Well, we got to cover in less 'n no time, an' when we got thar we found that the ravine was full an' runnin' over wi' mounted men. Among 'em was a man in a buggy, an' he was the one that done the talkin'.

"'Here, now,' he says, 'what ar' you fellers doin' in these diggin's, gallivantin' 'roun' wi' two fine nags an' a dog?'

"I never seed a sicker-lookin' man in all my born days than that man in the buggy. He was thin as a rail, an' his cheekbones stuck out like they was tryin' for to come through the skin. He was dark-complected to start wi', an' his skin was so yaller that it had a greenish look. Thar wa'n't nothin' well about him but his eyes, an' they was jest blazin'; I wanted to git behind a tree an' see ef they had made any holes in my cloze. I jest know'd he could see plum' through me. An' right then I made a good guess. Stidder salutin', I took off my hat.

"Says I: 'Gener'l Forrest, Colonel George Adair, of Atlanta, tol' me ef I seed you to give you his howdy.'

"A faint streak of a smile showed on his face.

"'Well, how is Adair?' he says.

"'Why, jest as full of fun as he was when a boy,' says I.

"Wi' that, I let him know in a mighty few words what we was arter, an' the way I said it, or the thing itself, kinder smoothed his feathers.

"'Well, who is this young feller wi'

the crutch, an' what kinder mettle is he got?' says the Gener'l.

"Wimberly Driscoll looked at him with a cute shake of the head an' a glance at the buggy.

"'I reckon you're right,' says the Gener'l; 'two cripples won't do much harm amongst a whole passel of healthy men.' He had been wounded in the foot, an' he could n't ride a hoss. He had his leg propped up in the rickety buggy so the blood would n't run in it, an' it was plain to see that the hurt had got the best on him.

"We give as good an account of ourselves as we know'd how, an' I reckon the Gener'l believed us, but somehow or other he wa'n't quite certain an' shore. Says he:

"'Thar's a passel of Yankees in the timber over yan, an' I want to find out a leetle more about 'em. Go out thar an' give 'em a dar'!'

"Now, I tell you," said Mr. Sanders, looking as solemn as he could, "I had a pillercase at home that had on it, 'Sweet dreams to thee,' an' I never wanted to lay my head on anything so bad in my life. It looked like I had a longin' for that pillercase an' the piller under it that nothin' else in the world 'd satisfy, an' I come mighty nigh statin' the whole case to the Gener'l; but Wimberly did n't give me time. He saluted like he wuz on parade, an' wheeled his mar', an' it seemed like I was in duty bound for to foller him. I went through purty much the same motions, an' the roan, bein' a kind of a smart Aleck, did n't need for to be spurred to foller the gray mar'.

"Wimberly Driscoll went in a canter, an' the roan had to foller suit. The pillercase faded from my mind, an' I reckon our sperrets riz as we felt the cool win' rushin' by. The houn' was runnin' along on the groun' some'rs nigh us, but he done like he know'd lots more than he did at fust. The roan had a stride long enough for to git him alon'-side the gray mar' wi'out any trouble, an' the minnit I got whar I could see Wimberly's face I know'd that his ancestry was whippin' an' spurrin' him on — the wild thing that was in their blood was b'ilin' in him. He 's the fust an' last man I ever seed that looked like he come out'n the book that has all that folderol in it about derrin'-do, an' nothin' about derrin'-don't. On horseback, he did n't no more look like a man wi' just one foot than he looked like a squinch-owl. He moved wi' the gray mar' jest like he was stitched to the saddle. I reckon ef I hadn't 'a' been feelin' right peart, the sight of Wimberly's face would 'a' holp me up might'ly.

"We had the hosses well in han', bekaze when you 're gwine whar you 're gwine, as the niggers say, 't ain't no use for to fling your young life away. Gallopin' to'rds the p'int of timber land, whar we supposed the enemy was, we soon come in sight of a whole passel on 'em on the furder side, whar the prairie land begun for to git in its work for miles an' miles, furder than the eye kin see. Some was mounted, some was manœuv'rin', an' away beyant 'em was the smoke of camp-fires. From the glimpse I ketched on it I judged that thar was mighty nigh a whole army some'rs in the neighborhood. We slowed up, an' then stopped, an' bimeby we started for to go back the way we come. The Bobby

Blues had sighted us about the time we seed 'em, an' they had no idee of lettin' us git away wi'out shakin' 'em by the han' an' axin' how the folks was.

"Some on 'em took a snap-shot as we turned, an' then come a reg'lar skirmish, all on the enemy's side. Half a dozen started arter us, an' thar may have been more, but I did n't wait for to count 'em. Three foller'd right arter us, an' three rode wide, like they was aimin' for to cut us off from the shelter of the timber. When he got a good chance Wimberly turned in his saddle, an' let his carbine speak a gentle word. I dunner whether the shot hit the man he aimed at, or whether it hit the nag he was ridin', but the next thing I seed the hoss was runnin' wild an' whickerin', the stirrups a-flyin', an' ever'thing lookin' our way. That was bekaze the loose hoss was constant a-runnin' betwixt us an' the Bobby Blues. They could n't 'a' ketched him ef they 'd 'a' had time, for, like all high-strung creeturs, sech as hosses an' wimmen, he was crazy bekaze he did n't have a man's han' for to show him what to do an' whar to go.

"The hunt led right by the ravine whar Gener'l Forrest was in ambush, ef you kin call it that, an' I ruther expected some of his men for to git in behind the Yanks an' cut 'em off from the'r command; but, so fur as I could see, he never shuck a limb. He jest let us ride right on to our doom, as they say in the books. Thar was five arter us — two comin' right along, an' three runnin' betwixt us an' the timber. I says to Wimberly:

"'We 've got to handle these fellers by our own lone selves, an' we 'd jest as well be up an' doin'.'

"All this time the rackin' roan had n't broke into a gallop. He jest rocked along on two legs at a time, as pacin' hosses will, givin' me e'en about as much satisfaction as a cradle wi' a saft piller in it. Wimberly nodded his head.

"'Now,' I says, 'when I give the word, turn the gray mar' to the right, an' I 'll whirl the racker to the left.' So said, so done. 'Now!' I said, when the time come. Our creeturs had been prepar'd for the move before they made it, an' wi' the word the thing was done! We had let the boys in blue gain on us, an' they had quit shootin', most likely bekaze they wanted to spar' the hosses.

"It puzzled us at the time, but we found out arterwards that they belonged to a fresh cavalry regiment from Chicago. I 've thought sence that ever'-thing would 'a' turned out the way it did ef they 'd 'a' been seasoned men. Nobody never gits seasoned to a big surprise, 'specially when they 're all keyed up expecting somethin' else to happen. Natchally, when we turned, one one way, an' another t' other, they did n't have time for to take off the'r hats; they did n't even have time for to look dignified; they was doin' all they could for to pull the'r creeturs in, an' they was purty busy wi' a lot of other things they had in the'r minds. Me an' Wimberly did n't have but one thing in the wide world to do, an' that was to ride right at 'em full tilt, an' take the chances that Providence maps out for the right kind of work, 'specially ef it 's done quick an' slick.

"I reely believe we 'd 'a' got the wust on it, anyhow, wi' two ag'in' two, ef it had n't but 'a' been for the gray mar'.

No sooner did she see the strange hosses sweepin' down to'rds her than she backed her y'ears so it looked like she did n't have none, an' fetched a loud squeal that sounded like a 'oman tryin' to walk a log over the creek. She run at the nighest hoss wi' open mouth, an' before a sheep could shake his tail we had the boys in blue huddled up together, wi' the'r hosses a-bitin' an' a-fightin' an' a-squealin'.

"They was two of the maddest men you ever seed in this errytatin' world. The'r faces was all puckered up, jest like schoolboys a-tusslin'. They had on sabres — you know how the cavalry use to show off wi' long sabres — but 't would 'a' been a heap better for 'em ef they 'd 'a' been armed wi' skillets. One feller did hit me across the head wi' his sabre, but it done him more harm than it done me, bekaze it made me mad, an' I jest grabbed him by the wrist, an' tried for to yerk his arm out'n the socket. At the same time, I roweled his hoss behind the fore shoulder wi' the big Mexican spur some of the boys had give me for a joke

"Betwixt backin' hoss an' pullin' man, the feller seed he was about to git in deep trouble, an' he says: 'Don't you know if you drag me off'n this hoss I'll git hurt?' The way he said it was what took me; he wa'n't no more skeered than I was, an' he spoke much like he would ef I'd 'a' been in his way in a crowd.

"I allowed that this was his fust taste of war, an' 't wa'n't no more like the kind of fightin' he'd read about in the books than a grist-mill is like a runaway hoss an' buggy. Before I could make answer, the hoss that the gray mar' was gnawin' give way in his hind legs an' went down in a flounder that come mighty nigh doin' as much damage as a shell of canister. I dunno how the roan kept his legs under him in the gener'l splash an' splutter, but he done like he was comfortable, an' he stood up to his work like a little man. All this time the boys in blue was hittin' at one another, an' cussin', an' the gray mar' was scrougin' an' squealin' like a creetur possessed. I helt on to my frien's han' tell he went down wi' the rest, an' by that time the war was over — I mean our little private war.

"You won't believe me, but all that me an' Wimberly had to do was to set on our hosses an' let the gray mar' do the business. Talk about football — why, football as it 's played at our Christian schools wa'n't a marker to that scrimmage; an' yet nobody got hurt! You never seed sech a sight in all your born days. Thar was a lot of fun at the bottom of it, an' I 've laughed myself to sleep many a time when I 'd think on it; but right then an' thar I could n't 'a' been more astonished at the outcome than ef I had ketched a sturgeon in a haystack.

"Jest as soon as I could gether up an' collect my seven senses out'n the elements whar they was floatin', I looked around for the three fellers that had rode wide tryin' for to cut us off. They was so busy wi' the idee they had in the'r minds that they never took the trouble for to watch the little rucus we had wi' the balance on 'em. They rode so close to Forrest's men that one or two on 'em rid out in the open an' axed 'em in out'n the rough weather. Purty soon arterwards one of the Gener'l's couriers rid out whar we could see him, waved his hands, an' motioned us for to go south.

"Well, we did n't need any strong invitation, bekaze the boys in blue on the timber ridge was sorter fixin' for to make a line of battle; they was watchin' us through glasses, an' one or two on 'em was gallopin' about wavin' the'r swords. We did n't want to be pepper'd wi' grapeshot, an' so we took our pris'ners an' meandered arter Forrest's reconnoit'rin' party. When we j'ined the Gener'l, a couple of hours later, he looked like he was might'ly holp up. His eyes had a fresh sparkle in 'em an' he looked like he was willin' for to smile ef he got a good chance. Nothin' would do but we must go to his headquarters, an' sech vittles as he had we got!

"'You nee'n' ter tell me, boys,' he says, 'that you don't know your business. Ef you 'd 'a' got to shootin' out thar in the open, we 'd 'a' had the whole caboodle right at our heels, an' we'd 'a' had to git out the best we could. I wish to Heaven that ten thousand sech fellers would ride up right now an' tell me Howdy-do! How 's George Adair?'

"Wi' that we got to talkin' about matters an' things fur from the war. I told him a few tales, sech as used to make the boys raise a yell, an' I reckon we had a right good time.

"We had to git back to the war somehow, an' along about that time the Gener'l was called on by some officers of the army, an' they begun for to talk about the battle that 'd be fit the next day. Gener'l Forrest was ready to fight, but he said that somebody else would have to take the responsibility. The blue boys was edgin' in on the Okolona bottoms, an' somethin' had to be done for to keep 'em from burnin' the supplies the Confederacy was dependin' on. That much was certain. But Gener'l Forrest was sick; he reely ought to 'a' been in bed; an' he jest told all an' singular that he would n't take no responsibility whar he could n't see his way cle'rer than he seed it then. An' so it went at that. The battle was fit, an' we was left jest a little bit wuss off than we was before. The Confederates could hold the Union army back, but they could n't run it out, an' 't was jest a question of time when the Yanks would send down another army as big as the one they had, an' jest run over ever'thing in sight. Mobile was in danger, or would be, an' things looked like they was gittin' in a shape to crumble from under our feet.

" Some of the officers that happened to

be on hand when me an' Wimberly was wa'n't so well acquainted wi' Gener'l Forrest hisself as they was wi' what he had done, an' so the talk meandered 'roun' to the way he done his fightin'. Some on 'em said 't was claimed by the papers that he had been usin' Bonaparte's tactics.

"'When it comes to that,' says the Gener'l, 'a heap of folks seem to have the idee that my front name is Napoleon Bonaparte, an' I reckon that's about as nigh as I git to his tactics. Ef you mean business, you want mighty little tactics — the less the better. A good hand wi' a pen kin write 'em all down in less 'n a minnit an' have time to spar'. You want to know what the other feller is aimin' at, which way he's comin', an' about what time he'll come, an' you want to git thar a little ahead on him, an', when he comes, raise a whoop an' a hurrah, an' make him believe you 've got the most men.

" 'Thar 's another p'int that ain't down in the books, I reckon: In any kind of a scrimmage, from the biggest battle to the littlest skirmish, thar allers comes a time when one side or the other, an' sometimes both, git the idee that they 've done e'en about all they kin do an' might as well quit. Thar 'll be a kind of wa-verin' — you may not see it, but you 'll know it. It comes like a flash, an' is gone before you kin snap your finger, an' right then is the time for to push things a little harder an' yell a little louder — an' the man that does that, he 's the feller that 'll whip the fight every time. You may call that the art of war, or not, jest as you please,' he says, 'but I 've never know'd it to fail.'

" One of the officers — I reckon from

the way he helt hisself he was a West P'inter — laughed an' said he could n't understand that.

"'Nuther kin I,' says the Gener'l as quick as lightnin'. 'When a fight 's gwine on, thar 's a heap of things I have to find out from my feelin's. Many a time I 've been as certain I was whipped as I am that I 'm talkin' to you; an' I knowed the other feller was feelin' the same way. Right then an' thar I order a charge, an' kick up a bigger racket than ever, an' the thing 's done.'

"Well, the talk went on for some time, an' then Forrest went in another room of the little cabin that was his headquarters, an' had a talk wi' some of the officers, an' jest as the door was shut I seed a guard comin' up wi' a ol' nigger man. Thar was a look about him that reminded me of home an' Jud Simmon's mammy-in-law.

I glanced at 'im ag'in, an' then I know'd it was Featherston's Drew.

"'Why, hello, Drew!' says I. 'What wind of docterin' blow'd you out here?'

"He was the gladdest in the world for to see me, an' then he seed Driscoll an' he was still gladder, bekaze Wimberly was a great favorite of his. He grinned an' vowed the sight of us made him feel like he was at home, walkin' along the street in the shade of the chanyberries. For Wimberly's sake I ast about Margaret Featherston, an' ol' Drew declared she was livelier than ever, an' he hinted that she was givin' some trouble to her Cousin Olivia Featherston.

"Arter a while Gener'l Forrest got rid of his visitors, an' come back to whar we wuz.

"'What are you doin' here?' he says to ol' Drew, lookin' like he was gwine to bite his head off — he never liked niggers, an' never trusted 'em.

" Drew said he was oblidze to go whar he was sent, more especially when his mistiss had sent him. Gener'l Forrest glared at 'im so quare that Drew turned to me, an' says:

" 'Marse Billy, please, suh, tell de Gener'l dat you know me!'

" Gener'l Forrest kinder smiled, but he was mighty blunt. 'What do you want wi' me?' he says.

" Wi' that ol' Drew fumbled around in all of his pockets, an' presently looked in the linin' of his hat an' pulled out a letter an' handed it to the Gener'l wi' a bow an' a scrape that 'd 'a' put a French dancin'-master to the blush.

" 'These wimmen!' says Gener'l Forrest, an' then he laughed, crammed the letter in his pocket, an' turned to the nig-

"'What are you doin' here?' he says to ol' Drew, lookin' like he was gwine to bite his head off"

ger an' ast him ten thousand questions. He made ol' Drew tell 'im all he know'd about things in an' around Memphis, all about the Featherstons, the soldiers sent to guard the place, an' who come an' who went, whar they come from an' whar they went to; an' then, when he had l'arnt all he could, he leaned back in his cheer an' looked at the rafters, an' said nary a word.

"Ol' Drew, squattin' down on the doorstep, begun for to talk to Wimberly about ol' times, the times when he was a young chap, an' the ol' nigger use to tote him around on his back; about the times when him an' Margaret Featherston used to be sweethearts. Drew declared that she had n't nigh forgot Marse Wimberly, an' then he laughed at somethin' in his mind. Says he:

"'Marse Wimberly, you ain't fergot

dat ar Mr. Bushrod Claiborne, is you? De man what you had a fight wid about de gray mar'? Well, suh, he comes dar constantly, an' it look like to me dat he 's drappin' his wing at Miss Margaret.'

"'What is Bushrod Claiborne doing with the Yanks?' says I.

"Somehow the name of Bushrod Claiborne appeared to rouse Gener'l Forrest from his doze, ef dozin' he was.

"'Bushrod Claiborne!' he says with an oath that mought 'a' come from one of the old-time prophecíers the Bible tells about, it was so big an' bitter. 'Why, I 'd ride forty — yes, fifty — mile to-night, sick as I am, ef I could lay hands on that man!' He did n't lose hisself in his thoughts no more. He called to one of his men, an' told him to take charge of ol' Drew. 'Make him help about the hosses, give him some supper, show him whar to sleep, an' fetch him here to me in the mornin'. Be certain you fetch him at daybreak!' Then he give us the wink for to go to bed.

"When I sleep, I sleep," said Mr. Sanders. "I reckon I make as much fuss as a freight ingine gwine up grade on a damp night, but that kinder thing don't pester me. I woke about day, an' raised up an' looked aroun'. A fire had been built out in the open an' some un was cookin' breakfust. Gener'l Forrest was settin' by the fire, an' right at his elbow was the ol' man, the daddy of the young 'oman whose misery an' misfortune had made a mighty bad half-hour for us — the young 'oman wi' the little child, who had cried so when she heern that Gener'l Forrest was dead.

"I woke Wimberly, an' in half a minute we had jumped into sech of our cloze as we had took off. Then we went to the fire, an' the Gener'l told us that Mr. Mooneyham would guide us whar he wanted us to go. The old man kinder shuffled around an' said he thought likely he had seed us before. He was one of Forrest's scouts, an' the Gener'l was sendin' him wi' us so 's he could fetch back some news that he wanted mighty bad to hear.

"'Ten to one,' he says to Mr. Mooneyham, 'you 'll see Bushrod Claiborne. Ef you do, jest let him alone. I want him to think that ever'thing is all right out your way. Ef you fool wi' him, he 'll be too much for you, an' you don't want to git in any more trouble on his account. Leave him to me; jest leave him to me; he 's my meat, an' I want to git my han's on him.'

"'I think,' says Wimberly, 'that he

either led or guided a party of raiders through Georgia jest about the time I made up my mind to come to you.'

"'Well, you can bet ever'thing you 've got,' says Gener'l Forrest, 'that he did n't do any leadin'; he ain't nothin' but a plain, ever'-day spy, an' the part fits him like a new suit of tailor-made cloze. I know 'd him before the war an' sence; in fact, he was one of my partners, an' he 's the fust white man that ever fooled me. I 've got a heap of things laid up ag'in' him, an' some of 'em is betwixt me an' this ol' man here. I 'll git my han's on him arter a while, an' when I do—' He just left it hangin' in the a'r, but thar wa'n't no sort of doubt what he 'd do. His temper was at a white heat ever' time he mentioned Bushrod Claiborne's name.

"'What I want you to do,' the Gener'l

says, when we was about ready for to start, 'is to see how things look around Memphis; I want you to see ef the letters I have been gittin' from that neighborhood are all correct. A heap depends on that, a heap more 'n I kin tell you right now, an' a heap depends on you-all. Mooneyham here will fetch me the news. You rickerlect how you used to choose sides in games when you was boys — a paddle marked wi' cross an' piles? Well, ef ever'thing is easy, an' the walkin' 's good, an' the gate not well 'tended, put a cross mark on a piece of paper an' give it to Mooneyham; ef ever'thing is all the other way, jest put three straight lines on the paper — I 'll know. I 'm a-gwine to give you a hoss for the nigger, for to kinder pay you back for the two you ketched yistiddy. Mooneyham is gwine wi' you, but sometimes he won't be in sight, an' you 'll have to do the best you kin. You 'll likely meet Captain William Forrest, or some of his men. Ef you do jest tell him that his sick brother is gittin' along as well as could be expected; this 'll be a clean bill of health for you, bekaze Brother William ain't what you might call a discriminatin' man; he won't ax you what church you belong to before he puts a hole or two in you.'

"Wi' that the Gener'l give us the so-long salute, an' done like he 'd ruther see our backs than our faces, though he told Mooneyham that he wanted him for to be mighty keerful on this trip. Well, off we put, the ol' man in the lead. It was mighty funny to me that he 'd ruther walk than ride, but he was made that-a-way, I reckon, an' ef so, he shorely was made right, for of all the walkers that ever I laid eyes on he was the out-doin'est. Ef he had any limit, I never seed 'im come to it. He 'd walk hard all day, an' when night come he was lots fresher than the hosses. When he wanted us to go fast, he 'd jest ketch a-holt of my stirrup, an' swing along like a man gwine arter the doctor.

"Thar 's a right smart piece of ground betwixt Massasip an' Memphis, 'specially the way we went. We had to keep to the cover of the big woods, an' then they did n't look like they was a bit too big. When we started off we felt kinder sorry for Mooneyham, but we had n't gone fur before we was sorry that we had been sorry. We jogged along, tryin' for to make it easy for him, an' he had to stop in the road an' wait for us.

"'Ef you travel like that,' he says, puckerin' up his mouth, 'you 'll git thar by next fall, an' much good it 'll do you,' says he. 'Two mile up the road you 'll come to a big white house wi' green blinds: turn in at the lot gate, but don't go in the lot — go round it ontell you come to the spring path. On the hill nigh the spring you 'll see a 'oman plattin' straw. The word is: "Good-mornin', ma'am, I hope you 're feelin' well arter the little spell you had. Will you show me the Mooneyham road?" — don't forgit — the Mooneyham road.' Wi' that he went into the bushes, an' out of sight same as ef he 'd splunged into the sea.

"We rid on, an' 't was jest as he said; thar was the 'oman settin' on a stump on the hill plattin' straw for to make a hat. She wa'n't ol' an' she wa'n't young, but she looked mighty quare. Wimberly give her the word.

" ' 'T ain't none of my business,' she says, wi' a pitiful smile, ' but it looks to me like it hain't no road for a youngster wi' a crutch an' a houn' dog.'

" She riz up, she did, an' then we seed she was a hunchback. She motioned us to foller an' she went slidin' an' glidin' through the woods wi' so little fuss that she put me in mind of the wild creeturs.

" 'T wa'n't long tell we come to whar a lanky, bar'footed boy, wi' a flint-an'-steel rifle, was lookin' up a tree like he was arter a squirrel. He scowled at us an' made as ef he would run off, but the 'oman coaxed him back. Says the 'oman:

" ' Squir'ls won't sp'ile while they is in the trees, Sugar. Make your purtiest bow, Sugar, an' then run an' show these gents to Winslett's cle'rin'.'

" The boy handed his rifle to the

'oman, an' put out through the woods like a hornet was arter him.

" 'Jest foller him,' says the 'oman, 'an' he'll take you whar you wanter go — Sugar will.'

"It was e'en about as much as we could do for to keep the boy in sight, yit, jest as we'd be about to lose him for good an' all, we'd come up wi' him. He'd uther be a-layin' flat on the groun', or he'd be a-dozing at the foot of a tree. As soon as we'd come up wi' him up he'd jump an' run on ahead. Ef we ever come to Winslett's cle'rin' I never know'd it. We did come to a cabin in the woods. Doors an' windows was shut, an' it looked as ef it mought be ha'nted. You know I don't believe in ghosts, but I know mighty well that thar's things so much like 'em that you could n't tell 'em apart ef you was to see 'em standin' side by side. The boy went aroun' the house, an' presently come back wi' a big basket, an' I allowed by the way Wimberly's houn' foller'd at his heels that the basket was full of vittles. Ol' Drew wanted to tote it for him, but the boy grinned an' shuck his head, as much as to say: 'You kin fool some folks, but you can't fool me!' Wi' this load he could n't go so fast, but he went fast enough.

"Purty soon we come up wi' Mooneyham. The ol' man was doin' so funny an' actin' so quare that I did n't know what to make on him. He was cussin' some, an' cryin' some, an' hittin' out in the a'r like he was in a reg'lar knock-down an' drag-out fight. He did n't stop when he seed us, but jest holler'd out:

"'Come here, gentermen! Come here an' look yan'! Thar goes Bushrod Claiborne as free as a bird! He passed right by me, an' I could 'a' retched out my han' an' drug him off'n his hoss — I could 'a' done it, but I did n't, an' now he 's a-gwine whar he 's a-gwine, wi' not a scratch on him — an' me a-standing here!'

"I never was as sorry for anybody in my life.

"It was funny the way Bushrod Claiborne bobbed up in front of us ever' time we turned aroun'. Ever'whar we went, it looked like we was uther on his trail or him on ours. We had come out on the big road, an' now we could see a man on horseback amblin' along a quarter of a mile away. His horse was a sorrel, wi' white hin' legs — a reg'lar stockin'-foot. Drew know'd the horse, an' Mooneyham know'd the man. The boy left us here, arter givin' the basket of vittles to Mr.

Mooneyham, an' all on us drapt back in the woods an' kep' on a-gwine north. We struck up wi' some of Captain Bill Forrest's men, an' they halted us for a while; but not for long did we stay wi' 'em.

" While he was talkin' to us word come that the offendin' Yanks was in sight, an' sech another scurryin' through the woods you never seed sence you was born. Cap'n Bill's Independents tried for to ride right over 'em. He did n't keer as much about tactics as his big brother. He jest went at the boys in blue like he was tryin' for to round up a stampeded drove of hogs an' mules, an' purty soon he had quite a sprinklin' of the Union folks.

" An' it reely was war, for the crackle of the guns, an' the gener'l racket an' riot, woke up both sides furder south, an' presently we could hear the boom-boom-along of the big guns on both sides, an' it sounded like things was gittin' purty well shuck up. When Cap'n Bill had finished his little job he took to the woods ag'in, an' the last we seed of him was right arter Mooneyham had told him about Bushrod Claiborne, an' he was cussin' so hard he like to 'a' fell off'n his hoss. I had to laugh, bekaze it was funny that you could n't call the feller's name in that part of the country wi'out makin' folks cuss ontell the a'r was blue.

"We went along, day arter day, amblin' an' ramblin' an' moseyin'. One night ol' Drew said he reckoned he 'd have to drap out'n the percession bekaze it would n't never do for his Miss Livvy to know he had been so fur south. He did n't belong to Miss Livvy, but him an' his mistiss an' his young mistiss was stayin' at her house. The next mornin' he wa'n't nowhar to be seen. Along about five o'clock in the arternoon we come to a mighty nice house on the edge of the woods. Mooneyham went up an' knocked like he 'd been thar before, an' purty soon he fetched us word that the folks was expectin' us. We did n't need no written invitation, bekaze we was dog-tired. In the house was two mighty nice ol' wimmen, an' a ol' man that looked mighty nigh as ol' as Methuselum. They had a nice hot meal of vittles for us. We was to stay thar all night, an' then, ever'-thin' bein' about ripe, Wimberly Driscoll was to go on to Graylands, a mile away, Drew was to take the gray mar' an' hide her out, whilst I was to leave the roan right whar he was, an' take my foot in my han' an' go wi' Mooneyham, changin' for the time bein' from a Georgy cracker to a Tennessee tacky.

"'T wa'n't no trouble for me to play the part, bekaze my cloze was about as shabby-lookin' as any set of men's gyar-ments you ever laid your eyes on.

"Well, we went, an' ever'thin' would 'a' fell out all right but for one or two things: a big Frenchy, a-fightin' for the Union on account of a bounty, an' the feller you 've heern tell on — Bushrod Claiborne."

III

Oh, what is the sickening shadow that swings in the field of the sun?
The wind from the Southland whispers, "His race is surely run!"
And the west wind sighs in answer, "The days of his years are done!"

— *Herndon's Ballad of the Spy.*

"I HAD N'T hardly got to Graylands, as folks called the place, before I seed that thar was somethin' wrong somewhar. Some things you kin see, some things you kin feel, an' some things you kin guess at; an' them that know'd me allers said I was a purty good guesser. Fust an' fo'most thar was that Frenchman from somewhar in Canada. He allowed that he did n't keer a continental for the Union, but he had a good chance to make a right smart little pile by j'inin' the army an' gittin' the big bounty they was payin' for recruits. He tried hard for to pull the wool over my eyes, but the plain truth was that he could n't fool me, an' I know'd by a little grin that hung aroun' the corners of his mouth that I could n't fool him. To hear him try to talk you 'd think he was a simpleton, but I never struck up wi' a much smarter man. He had been put thar for to look arter the place, an' the way he done it would 'a' pleased you. He 'd be readin' a little book he had, an' all of a sudden he 'd jump up, git his gun, rush around in front of the house and wave away a lot of stragglin' Yankees. It seemed like he could smell 'em a-comin'.

"I had n't been thar long before I got the lay of the land, but I could n't git it out'n my head that Frenchy know'd purty well what was in my min'. Maybe I give him too high a ratin', but I 'll never believe it. Anyhow, it done me no harm for to think so, bekaze I was keerful not to raise the curtain on any of our plans when he was around. He ax'd me one day why I did n't go to Memphis. Now, me an' Mooneyham had laid off for to go that very day, an' I wonder'd how Frenchy had drapt on the plan. I never let on, but you can take oath that I did n't go nigh Memphis that day, nor the next, an' when me an' Mooneyham did go, it wuz like havin' a spell of sickness.

"But Frenchy wa'n't the only trouble. The other one was love. Jest think on it! Nothin' but plain ever'-day love — the kind you read about in books, whar male an' female look at one another two or three times an' think they are betrothed, an' arter that they 've got for to have a twistin'-place! Ain't that the word? I may git it wrong, but it sounds that-a-way. You never seed two lovers that they wa'n't betrothed, an' did n't have a twistin'-place, an' wa'n't gwine roun' moonin' an' swoonin', an' thinkin' ever' minnit was gwine ter be the next. This was the case wi' Wimberly an' Margaret Featherston. She did n't know he was comin', an' arter he come she would n't hardly speak to him bekaze he had lost a foot. He sot in the parlor waitin' for her, an' she slipped down to the settin'-room an' peeped in, an' when she seed he had a crutch in place of a foot, she took the studs an' kinder balked; an' Wimberly, knowin' that she had seed him, waited a few minnits, an' when she did n't come, he riz an' was for gwine out'n the house an' never comin' back ag'in, an' then she run an' ketched him by his coat-tails, an' ax'd him ef that was what he come for, jest to let her see him an' then go off wi'out a word? An' how could he, of all men, be so cold an' so cruel?

"When Wimberly confided all this to me, an' sucked in his breath a time or two jest like he'd escaped the gallows, I like to 'a' lost my breakfast, an' I ax'd him for goodness' sake not to tell me any more sech stuff. I reckon he must 'a' been kinder hurt at me, but I could n't help that. Love that ain't got a stomach for pot-licker an' collards don't go fur wi' me, bekaze I never seed a 'oman that I'd sigh arter an' swaller my goozle fer. You kin count on three fingers the dif-f'unt kind of wimmen thar is in the world, an' when you're done countin' you can't tell t'other from which, they're all so much alike. I ain't never been so young that arry one on 'em or all on 'em could fool me, an' it speaks well for 'em that none on 'em ever tried.

"Now, don't go off an' say that I 'm abusin' the seck, bekaze I ain't. I like 'em all, but I ain't never had time to play like I was in love wi' 'em, or that I 'd go into the gallopin' consumption ef one on 'em showed me the back of her hand. Take Margaret's cousin, Miss Olivia — I never seed a finer 'oman than what she was. Thar wa'n't nothin' in the roun' world that she wa'n't up to date in. In age she must 'a' been hov'rin' roun' twenty-eight or thirty, an' yit she was as purty as Margaret, an' as lively. She had n't said two words to me before I seed that her two Georgia cousins had got to be a consider'ble burden on her han's. She was not only afear'd on 'em, she was afear'd for 'em; she was afear'd they 'd do or say somethin' that 'd git 'em in trouble. I judge that both Margaret an' her mammy had been sayin' things they ought not to. I never seed more 'n a half a dozen wimmen that could control the'r tongues, an' they was born deaf an' dumb, an' I reckon that, fust an' last, thar had been some right purty quarrels, all in a good humor, but leavin' a little sting here an' thar that rankled an' burnt. One for the Union an' the other two for secession! Don't you know they had a high ol' time, an' all on 'em a-pertendin' they was carryin' off a big joke!

"Ef ever'thing had 'a' been all right betwixt 'em, Wimberly Driscoll would never 'a' got a letter by way of Baylor's mail; an' when Miss Olivia, wi' her black hair an' laughin' eyes, declar'd she hated for to see 'em go, an' what a nice, happy time they 'd all had together, I put down naught an' added two ciphers for to make it look big. Miss Olivia went about fixin' for to git 'em off'n her han's as quick as she could. She ax'd some of the officers to dinner, an' opened her last bottle of claret for to git 'em in a good humor. What wi' the wine an' her clever tongue, the job was done. The officers said they 'd do ever'thing she wanted done, furnish a escort as fur as the'r lines went, an' pass through any frien's the ladies mought have. This was all she wanted, an' she done like a big load had been lifted from her shoulders.

"Wimberly Driscoll dined wi' 'em, but me an' ol' man Mooneyham kinder kept out'n sight. The background was for us, as you may say. That arternoon I mentioned to Mooneyham that we 'd better crack the Memphis hick'ry-nut an' see ef thar was any goody in it for Gener'l Forrest. He had a basket of eggs, an' I had another, an' we slipped off, as we thought, an' started to town. We had n't gone fur before I got the idee that we wa'n't gwine to git thar. We run right up on the big Frenchy I told you about. He was settin' down by a tree, his gun across his lap, a-readin' his little book. Thar ain't nothin' safer than a bluff, an' I was mighty much afear'd that this would n't work wi' Frenchy. We wa'n't in no road, the trees had been thinned out so that what had been a thick piece of timberland now looked like a park. I let Mooneyham git a leetle ahead, an' then I holler'd at him.

"'Hey!' I says, talkin' loud like he was deaf, 'maybe we can sell our eggs right here an' save the walk to town!'

"Mooneyham ketched right on like a hongry fish at a butterfly bait; he flung one han' up to his y'ear:

"'What 'd you say? Did n't I hear you speak?'

"I holler'd at 'im ag'in, a leetle louder.

"'Them eggs ain't for sale,' he says; 'they 've done been paid for by Colonel What 's-his-name.' He got the name off all right, but I disremember what it was. The Frenchman give me the cutest look I ever seed on a grown man's face. His smile was fetchin', as he remarked that he 'd like mighty well for to see the pullets that laid the eggs. It took me ontell the next day to understand what he said, his lingo was so furrin', but that did n't bother me a bit. I hollers to Mooneyham. says I:

"'He don't want no eggs; he wants to buy some settin' hens ef you got any. He wants 'em good an' ripe. He says he 'll give you seven dollars apiece for the kind of hens he wants.'

"Mooneyham looked at Frenchy like he was in a circus cage.

"So I holler'd out ag'in: 'He says he don't keer ef they 're bony an' feverish; that 's the way he likes 'em.'

"By this time Frenchy was as much in the dark about what I was sayin' as I was about his lingo. He shook his head; he know'd somethin' was wrong, but he did n't know what. He put his little book in his pocket, picked up his gun an' riz to his feet, an' made as ef he was gwine wi' us. When bluff meets bluff, thar 's allers fun for the onlooker. I shuck han's wi' Frenchy, an' said I 'd be the gladdest in the world ef he 'd come along, an' kinder keep his eye on me, bekaze I was afear'd of gittin' lost. I know'd mighty well he could n't go all the way, an' so I took him by the arm an' made believe for to help him along. 'An' when he come to the bound'ry of his beat, an' stopped, I stopped too, an' tried hard for to persuade him to come on.

"Well, he could n't come, but he wa'n't fooled; he know'd thar was somethin' up, an' he know'd that I know'd it. It 's powerful errytatin' for to be in that kind of fix, but Frenchy never let on. You 'd 'a' thought he was in the best humor in the world. My bluff chanced to be the biggest, an' it worked out like I thought it would, but ef he 'd 'a' had jest one comrade wi' him, whar would I 'a' been? Ef you kin figger it out, I wish you would; I 've tried many a time, but I never could git the right answer.

"Well, not to put ten words whar one oughter be, me an' Mooneyham went on to Memphis, an' found ever'thing wide open. Men that ought to 'a' been watchin' out for things was a-playin' sev'n up, an' ever'body looked like they was as happy as a rustyback lizard in the sunshine. I had n't been in the town ten minnits before I seed all that Gener'l Forrest wanted to know, an' when I come out wi' Mooneyham, I tol' him he 'd better start right back an' tell the Gener'l for to come on, an' be quick about it.

"When it come to Cross-an'-Piles, the sign was cross, an' so I jest took a piece of paper, draw'd a circle on it, an' made a cross mark on the inside. Wi' this in his pocket, Mooneyham started south ag'in, an' I know'd he 'd make time — 'Bekaze,' says I, 'you may ketch Bushrod Claiborne.'

"He fetched a little shiver, wi' 'The Lord send it!' says he.

"Well, arter the dinin' she give the officers, Miss Olivia had things purty much her own way. She tuck a notion, at the last minnit, that she 'd go wi' her cousins a part of the way, an' nothin' would do but Frenchy was to go wi' her. The commander at Memphis was to choose a man, she was to choose another, an' from Memphis would come transportation for the ladies. We was to go south for four or five miles, an' then cut across Tennessee ontell we got to Chattanooga, an' arter that we 'd have to trust to luck. That 's what we was to do. What we done was about as much like what we laid off to do as a cowcumber is like a watermillion.

"Fust an' fo'most come the dilly-dallyin'; the wimmen could n't hardly make up the'r minds to leave, though this was percisely what they was a-dyin' to do. They cousined an' cousined like a swarm of spring muskeeters. An' when the wimmen got good an' ready the officers that was to furnish the escort would put it off, an' when the officers was ready the wimmen foun' somethin' else to do. An' so it went, bubblin' up one day an' coolin' off the next, like a pot on a porely-fed fire. I tell you I was plum' outdone. I 'd as lief tried to skin a hummin'-bird wi'out losin' a feather. On top of that, when we all got ready, Wimberly Driscoll's gray mar' could n't be found high nor low. Drew had hid her out some'rs, an' when he went for to feed 'em that mornin' the gray mar' was gone. He had sense enough for to run an' git the rackin' roan.

"When he came for to tell me about it, he fetched the roan, an' Wimberly's houn' come wi' 'im, an' the idee struck me that maybe the dog could find the mar' better than any on us, 'specially as he begun to whine when he seed the roan all saddled an' ready for to go. Thar wa'n't no other chance, so I called to the houn' an' we went to whar Drew had hid 'er. I waved my han' at the dog, wi' a cry of 'Try for 'im, ol' fel'!' an' in less 'n no time he was runnin' down the road in full cry. He foller'd the road about a mile, lost the trail, an' then picked it up ag'in at a place whar the bars of a fence was down. We humped along like we was arter a red fox, an' by the time we had gone another mile or more — it mought 'a' been furder — I seed a feller in a uniform of blue comin' my way, ridin' a hoss an' leadin' the gray mar'. I had the funniest feelin' in the world when the man got close enough for me to take a good look at him. The minnit I seed him, I know'd it was Bushrod Claiborne, an' I was warm to his little game. I know'd he had tried to steal the gray mar', an' I know'd the tale he 'd tell. I seed that he know'd me, but he did n't let on, an' nuther did I. He had grow'd a big black beard sence I seed him last, but I 'd 'a' know'd him ef he 'd 'a' had his head in a bag.

"You 'll read in books that the meanness of folks allers shows in the'r faces, but don't you nigh believe it. Bushrod Claiborne was as handsome a chap as you 'd want to see, tall an' clean-lookin'. Innocence shone in his eyes, an' he had the slick look that you sometimes see in preachers. I says:

"'I thank you kindly, friend; you 've saved me considerbul trouble this day, an' I wish I could pay you back as you ought to be paid!'

"He rid right up to me an' tetched me on the arm. Says he:

"'Don't say a word! I 've had trouble

ketchin' this creetur, but it 's in the line of duty. I 've got to conduct a party south, an' when I got close to whar they was, I seed this mar' runnin' wild, an' I tried for to ketch her. You see for yourself whar she carried me.'

" 'Yes,' says I, 'she 's a funny creetur. In some of her ways she 's mighty like a 'oman.' But I thought to myself: 'You 're the biggest liar outside of Satan's dominions!'

" 'Why,' he says, 'I tried for to ride her, but I mought as well tried to ride the nor'west win'.'

"We both ambled back, narry one on us lettin' on that he know'd the other. But somehow I was might'ly holp up; he had tried for to steal the gray mar' an' got ketched, an' I thought it was a good sign, but I tell you right now, it come mighty nigh failin', like weather-signs fail in time of a long drouth. I dunno how Bushrod had come to be our escort. The wimmen all seemed to be happy over it, an' ef Wimberly Driscoll wa'n't happy over it, he did n't show it. The funny part about it was that Miss Olivia know'd that Claiborne was a Union spy, an' Margaret an' her mammy know'd that he was a Confederate spy. They had never mixed the'r knowledge in the same bowl; they was tryin' for to hide from one another what the man reely was, an' none of 'em know'd that he was the blackest rascal on top of the ground.

"I never let on about Claiborne tryin' for to steal Wimberly's hoss; all I said was that we had a mighty hard time tryin' for to ketch the gray mar' arter she got away. When me an' Claiborne got back, it was most too late for to make an early start, an' so we put off gwine ontell the next mornin'. I was sorter glad we did, for late that night, arter ever'body but me an' the Frenchman was in bed, we heern a mighty racket on the big road, an' I know'd then that Mooneyham had took back the news an' that Gener'l Forrest was raidin' the town. Frenchy ax'd me what the fuss was.

"'Well,' says I, 'it can't be a windstorm, bekaze thar ain't a cloud in the sky. Don' you reckon it's about time for Gener'l Forrest for to come up an' see his ol' Memphis friends? Don't you rickerlect the time when he use to live thar an' manage things for the boys?'

"Wi' that Frenchy flung his two han's in the a'r, an' said he had told his captain jest the day before that ef the Confederates wanted to run in on the Memphis garrison, thar wa'n't nothin' in the world for to hender 'em. He seemed to be glad that he was sech a talented prophet, bekaze he laughed so he had to hold his sides. Says he:

"'Doze gener'ls, doze gener'ls! I bet you dey no laugh!'

"Purty soon we heard the muskets a-cracklin', an' men a-hollerin', an' then the fox-hunt yell, an' I know'd that Captain Bill Forrest was havin' the time of his life. The fuss must 'a' woke Bushrod Claiborne, for presently he come a-stumblin' out'n the house, his beard tangled, an' his hat on crossways.

"'Barnum,' he says to the Frenchman, 'what's up in town? What's the row?'

"Frenchy flung up his han's an' shook his head.

"'As nigh as I can guess,' I says,

'Gener'l Forrest has come arter some fresh hosses, an' some cloth for to make his men some britches.'

"Well, sirs, you could 'a' brained him wi' a feather!

"'Gener'l Forrest!' he says. 'Why, shorely not — shorely not!'

"'It's him,' says I, 'an' not only that, but a man named Mooneyham is runnin' up an' down the big road down yander wi' gun an' knife, a-huntin' for a man that ought to be his daughter's husband. I tol' him that all the single men at this hotel was married, an' he went on up the road bellerin' like a town bull. I pity the folks whar he went along, bekaze they won't git no more sleep this night!'

"He sucked in a long breath, an' stood wi' his back to me while you could count ten, an' then he turned round wi' his face all screwed up like he had a mortal big pain in his stomach.

"'We must move,' he says; 'we must git away from here!'

"'What's the hurry?' says I. 'Ef Gener'l Forrest ain't afear'd of me, I know mighty well I ain't afear'd of him. I've heern so much about him I'd like to see him. Do you reckon he'd stand while I put my han' on him?'

"He did n't say a word about that, but I could see that he was skeer'd mighty nigh to death. You may say what you please, but they ain't no more pitiful sight than to see a grown man reely skeer'd. Death is purty bad, but it's ca'm: it ain't a marker to a skeer'd grown man.

"'I tell you,' he says, 'we've got to git away from here.' Then he stopped, an' presently, says he: 'It jest can't be Forrest! He could n't 'a' made the trip!

But, all the same, we 've got to git out of here.'

"'From the way you talk,' says I, 'you must be mighty well acquainted wi' Forrest.'

"'Why, we use to be partners before the war,' says he, 'an' we went in together. I jest don't want him to ketch me here when he thinks I 'm some'rs else.'

"Well, sirs, hosses could n't 'a' helt him back! He was in a panic ef ever you seed a man in one. He 'd 'a' had a chill ef he had 'a' heern a hoss gallopin' in the dark. He rousted out the folks, an', by good daylight, we was on our way south, the wimmen in a carryall which was drug along the road by two broke-down army mules. Miss Olivia was wi' 'em an' she had fixed things up so that Frenchy went along as the second escort.

He was a great big blondy feller, blue-eyed an' baby-lookin'. Miss Olivia was black-haired an' bright-eyed, an' I had the idee that both on 'em had got so use to one another that brighty liked blondy an' blondy liked brighty. That 's the way I put it down; the world kin git in a wrangle, an' pull ha'r an' spill blood, but they ain't no way for to keep the sandy-haired man or 'oman from the dark-complected. Think it over, an' ef you find out diffunt, send me a telegraph, freight to be paid at my end of the line. Wimberly was dark, an' Margaret Featherston was light, though in this day an' time they 're mostly of a muchness.

"It was quite a whet before we heern tell how Forrest come out, but you all know the tale now — privates on a stampede, gener'ls runnin' about the streets in the'r shirt-tails, an' a kind of a wild skeer blowin' about in the a'r. You may laugh at all this, but ef you was in bed, dreamin' of the nice things that comes to you in your sleep, an' a wild hullabaloo was to break loose under your window, sensible folks would excuse you for losin' your head, an' snaggin' yourself in the tender places tryin' for to git away from thar. I never laugh loud at folks that do percisely what I 'd 'a' done.

"The man I 'm a-laughin' at these days is about the size an' weight of William H. Sanders, aforesaid. For many a long year I was hot mad at him for bein' anybody's fool, but, as time went on, I got so I could sleep comfertubbly in the same bed wi' 'im. Now, the trouble was that what was done wa'n't done in the dark; I had on my fur-seein' specks; an' I know'd a thing or two that nobody thought I know'd. I know'd that Bushrod Claiborne was the grandest rascal in Tennessee; I know'd that I had ketched him tryin' for to steal Driscoll's gray mar'; I know'd that he was ever'thing that Gener'l Forrest said he was; an' yit, in the face of that, I let him put a blanket over my head an' ride me into the wild-woods. As we went along Frenchy rid by the carriage, ef you could call it a carriage, an' Bushrod Claiborne rid fust by me, an' then by Wimberly Driscoll; an' I 'll tell you the honest truth, honey wa'n't sweeter than that man's daily walk an' conversation.

"He had a tale to tell an' he tol' it, an' he ketched me wi' it as slick as stewed okry. Ever'body, he said, was down on him, an' allers had been, an' ef he was mean this was the reason. He 'd do a man a good turn, an' it 'd turn out to be a bad un; an' somethin' or other or somebody was allers comin' betwixt him an' what he wanted to do. It had been that-a-way ever sence he was a boy; when he 'd turn his han' to good, it 'd turn out for to be bad; an' when some un else 'd come along an' do the very same thing, it 'd turn out to be the best thing in the world. Day arter day he 'd tell about his misfortunes, an' he 'd deal wi' 'em in a way that made him out to be the wust-treated man in the world, sufferin' jest bekaze he was better 'n other folks. Talk was jest as easy to him as drawin' molasses from a hogshead on a hot day, an' it was the kinder talk that eats its way into your vitals, like grubs in a plow-hoss. I know'd he was lyin' jest as well as I know'd I was ridin' along wi' him; but he built up in my mind a kind of a Bible pictur' of a lonesome an' long-sufferin' martyr. He had been fed to the lions like a pan of dough to a pen of Shanghai chickens, an' he had got away by the skin of his teeth.

"He 'd 'a' made a good preacher ef thar ever was one, an' he 'd 'a' made ever' sinner in the bunch march weepin' to the mourners' bench. You may think that ain't so, but I tell you right now, it 's as true as the Gospel. The feller had a way about him that you could n't run away from. He 'd seize you by the belief, same as ketchin' a pig by the tail, an' you could n't git away to save your life. We went along slow, as I tol' you, an' by the time we got to Murfreesboro, me an' him an' Driscoll was as chummy as nine young squirrels in the same holler. Jest about the time we got thar, it was gittin' kinder dark. Frenchy was stickin' close to the wimmen, an' we was ridin' a little ahead of the mules. I noticed that somethin' or 'nother was worryin' Bushrod Claiborne, an' he looked so pale in the twilight, an' so low-spirited, that I kinder felt sorry for him, an' I up an' ax'd him what the trouble was.

"'Nothin' much,' says he; 'the times is sech that we 're all bound for to have our sheer of trouble, an' it sometimes happens that a feller has to play a double part. Some on 'em in this garrison knows me, an' they think I 'm wi' 'em heart an' soul. Somethin' tells me that I 'm likely to be ketched here, an' I want you two to know jest how it is. Ef anything happens to me, an' you should see Gener'l Forrest, jest tell 'im that I done my duty to the last!' I must 'a' made some fuss in my goozle, bekaze he kinder smiled an' shuck his head. 'Oh, I don't doubt you have heern him cuss me out, an' ef you 'd 'a' run across his brother Bill you 'd 'a' heern cussin' that was still wuss. But I don't mind that; it 's a part of the game. I 'm actin' for Gener'l Forrest, an' I can go furder an' do more ef ever'-body is of the belief that he hates me wuss 'n he hates a snake. In a way, I can carry out his wishes an' desires lots better.

"'But I feel like I 'm a-gwine to git ketched up wi' right in this town,' he says. 'I 've got on the'r cussed uniform, an' I 'm a-carryin' in my pockets a lot of papers that 'll do the business for me ef they 're found on me. Ef I had cloze on like you fellers, wi' passports signed by the commander at Memphis, I 'd have some chance, but I 've been wi' these Yankees for some months, gath-erin' information that Gener'l Forrest would give a purty to git. I reely dunno what to do about 'em; I reckon I better leave 'em in the keer of the ladies,' he says.

"Well, this kinder got my dander up, an' I says, says I: 'You don't want to have the wimmen hung up as spies, do you?'

"'Oh,' says he, 'they 'd be safe enough. Ef the wust come to the wust, they could say whar they got 'em. But nobody won't think about papers. I tell you right now,' he says, 'I would n't give that'—he snapped his fingers—'for what becomes of me, but I want them papers for to git to Gener'l Forrest, an' ef you fellers will undertake to git 'em to him, no matter what happens to me, he 'll be the happiest man you ever seed, an' I think they 'll be safest wi' the wimmen.'

"One of Wimberly Driscoll's auntcestors spoke up at that, usin' Wimberly's mouth an' tongue. He ripped out the wust oath I ever heern him use, an' says he:

"'Gi' me the papers; I'll take 'em. Do you reckon I'd let you git the ladies in trouble?'

"Bushrod Claiborne kinder hung his head at this. Says he:

"'I'll give 'em to you, but they'd be safer wi' the wimmen, an' the wimmen would be safe, too. I give both on you fair warnin' that ef the Yankees find 'em on you they ain't nothin' in the round world kin save you.'

"I took notice, though, that he was in a mighty big hurry for to give Wimberly the papers. To have so much damage in 'em thar was mighty few on 'em. I made Wimberly divide wi' me, an' in ten minnits we had done forgot about 'em.

"We rid into Murfreesboro, show'd

our passes, found 'em all right, seed that the wimmen was stow'd away all right, an' got a place for the men folks for to sleep. Me an' Wimberly was dead tired, an' we did n't wait for Bushrod Claiborne to come in before we tumbled down on our humble pallets, which was the best accommodation we could git. I fell right to sleep like a log in a mill-pon' an' floated around on dreams of home for quite a considerbul spell. Sometime endurin' of the night — it mought 'a' been day for all I know'd — I woke up kinder sudden like, an' I know'd by that that somethin' or other was gwine on. I did n't move, but lay thar as still as a cat a-watchin' for mice.

"Arter a while I heern feet a-shufflin' jest outside the door, an' then whisperin'. Then a knock on the door, a good-sized bang. Says I, 'Don't knock so loud on a true believer's door, but jest come right in.' The door was flung open, an' thar stood a boy in blue, wi' a file of soldiers — I could see the'r feet behind him. The officer wa'n't none too polite, I can tell you! He ordered me aroun' like he was the boss of sixteen continents.

"'We want you an' your friend,' he says. 'Git right up an' put on your cloze.' He punched Wimberly in the short ribs wi' the scabbard of his sword, an' tol' him the same.

"We flung on our gyarments, sech as we had tuck off, an' then they went through us, fust lookin' under the pallets, an' shakin' out the bedcloze. They did n't have no trouble in findin' the papers that Bushrod Claiborne had give us, bekaze they wa'n't hid, an' when they had read 'em they looked at us like they was sorry.

"Says I: 'Be keerful wi' them papers, bekaze they belong to Bushrod Claiborne, the biggest rascal in the whole divid'd nation.'

"The officer kinder smiled a sad little smile, winked at the ceilin', an' then says he: 'You'll have to go wi' us.'

"'Ef it's a case of havin' to,' says I, 'we can't put it off ontell Christmas.'

"I tried for to be gay and light-hearted, but I know'd mighty well we was in for it. Bushrod's whole scheme appeared before my eyes like it was writ on the wall, an' ef we was in for it, 't was our own fault an' nobody else's. He wanted Margaret Featherston, an' he know'd he did n't have no chance while Wimberly Driscoll, crippled as he was, was on top of the ground. He had set a trap for us, an' we had walked right in it wi' our eyes open. You may read in books that folks is holp up, when the wust comes to the wust, by patr'otism, an' princerple an' all them kinder doin's, but don't you b'lieve it. When we was hauled up before the court-martial, an' ax'd nine thousand questions, I did n't feel no diffunt from the rest of the malefactors that have been swung up, an' draw'd an' quartered an' disboweled. Our trial did n't last long, bekaze we did n't have no case. All the facts was dead ag'in' us. Thar was the papers found warm in our cloze. All we could say was that we got 'em from Bushrod Claiborne, who said he was actin' for Forrest. An' Claiborne did n't take the trouble to make denials; he jest laughed at us like he would at circus clowns.

"I allow," Mr. Sanders went on, rubbing his chin, "that none of you fellers ever had occasion to set up wi' your thoughts — your complexions don't look like it. Yit it 's good to have to go through it ef you kin come out all right. It 'll take all the starch an' stiffenin' out of you, an' never ag'in while the worl' stan's will you take the notion that you 're a little better than some un else. Well, we was tried, convicted, an' sentenced for to be hung at half-past seven the second day — we had jest forty-eight hours to set up wi' ourselves. Wimberly had some gold pieces in his cloze, an' I had a few. He wanted me to take 'em an' clear out ef I could. Bein' crippled, he had no chance to git away. I reckon maybe we could 'a' bought the jailer, ef the jailer had n't 'a' been Bushrod Claiborne. I found that out by rappin' at the door ontell they opened it, an' thar was Claiborne lookin' as pious as a circuit rider.

"'What do you want?' says he.

"Says I: 'I did want to speak to a white man'—an' then I turned away. He tried hard for to find out what I wanted, but narry one on us would look at 'im, much less speak to him.

"It ain't no use to tell you about our thoughts when we was left by ourselves. Time went by, as time will, an' the mornin' come when we was to walk on air. Considerin' ever'thing, we wa'n't feelin' so bad. I tried, an' found that I could crack a joke jest as well as I kin now, an' Wimberly Driscoll could laugh at it jest as loud as he ever did. A man fetched our breakfust about six, an' put it down mighty solemn-like.

"'Thank you, friend,' says I; 'you're comin' to the funer'l, I hope?' He stood an' stared at us, an' shook his head.

'Ax all the boys,' says I, 'an' give us a good send-off.'

"The man went out like he was skeer'd, the door slammed on us, an', funny as it may sound, that was the last I saw of the man or anybody like him.

"Whilst I was chawin' on my hard-tack, I took notice that ever'thing was still as death in the hallway of the jail whar the gyuards was allers playin' seven-up or poker. An' then, about a mile away, come the boom-along of a ten-pounder. Then we could hear folks runnin' aroun' an' about, an' hosses a-gallopin'. Then ever'thing was still ag'in for a right smart whet. I know'd somethin' was gwine on, an' so did Wimberly; we know'd it so well that what little appetite we had left us, an' we sot thar starin' at one another like two boys kept in arter school. Then we heern a trumpet sing, an' though I never heern it but twice before in my life, I 'd 'a' know'd it ef I 'd 'a' heern it in the next worl'.

"'Wimberly,' says I, 'that 's Gaus! Nobody else kin blow a brass horn that-a-way, an' I 'll bet you Gener'l Forrest ain't ten feet away from him!'

"Well, thar we was, locked up in jail. The windows was too high for us to see what was gwine on, but we know'd thar was some kind of hullabaloo a-brewin'. Presently we heern some un rushin' up the steps — we was in the second story of the jail building — an' then some un holler'd out:

"'Better git away whilst you can! That devil Forrest is takin' the town, an' ef he finds you here, nothin' will save you!'

"The voice belonged to Bushrod Claiborne, an' I 'd 'a' know'd it ef I 'd 'a' heern it in the northermost part of Rooshy wi' a South American harrycane blowin' the snow a mile high! Wimberly Driscoll know'd him, too, an' holler'd at him, darin' him to open the door, an' callin' him all the names calcalated to make a man fight.

"Claiborne never answered a word ontell all the gyuards had run off, an' then he laughed an' says:

"'I 'm a-gwine for to give you two fellers a taste of hell before you git thar!'

"Wi' that we heern him a-rattlin' paper, an' presently we seed smoke a-comin' under the door, an' then we know'd that he was fixin' for to give us a purty warm time. The jail wa'n't nothin' but a barn as to age; one of the sills had rotted away clean across the middle an' the floor was a-saggin'.

Bushrod Claiborne lit his paper an' shoved it in between the een's of the planks an' under them. I says to Wimberly:

"'Thar ain't nothin' that kin save us this time, ol' feller, short of Providence, an' I reckon we might as well make up our minds that our time 's come.'

"He laughed, an' says he: 'It 's all right, ol' friend; you 've been mighty good to me, fust an' last, an' I hate to see you caged up in this hole on my account. Ef you do git out, an' I don't, you know whar to go an' who to take keer on.'

"We heern some un run up the steps, then another, an' arter a while two or three. Then some un belched out an oath that would 'a' blistered ef it had 'a' hit anybody, an' I know'd that Gener'l Forrest was right out thar at the door.

"'Some of you lousy scounderls run an' git me an ax, an' be quick about it!'

"He growled an' growled an' cussed ontell the ax come, then he beller'd out:

"'Stan' back from the door, whoever you are!' Well, we stood back, an' then he hit the door a whack that shuck the whole buildin', an' he kep' on a-hittin' ontell the lock flew off an' the door come open.

"I wish you could 'a' seed Gener'l Forrest as I seed him then. His face was right purple, an' the veins in the side of his neck stood out like they was swelled, an' his eyes was red as blood. I know'd then why ever'body was afear'd of him; ef ever a man looked like a demon he did. I believe ef he'd 'a' blow'd out a long breath you could 'a' seed it smoke! He ripped out a big oath, wi' 'Ef I'd 'a' been a minnit later they'd 'a' had you whar they wanted you! I 'll make 'em pay for this! Ever' man concerned in this will wish he 'd never been born!' Nuther before nor sence have I ever seed a man so stirred up!

"Says I: ''T wa'n't the Yankees, Gener'l. They had fixed up for to hang us as spies all right, but Bushrod Claiborne was at the bottom of it, an' when he found out that you had took the town he was keen for to roast us alive.'

"Well, all the pris'ners that had been took in the garrison was lined up before you could use your han'kcher an' put it back in your pocket ag'in. All the'r names was took down in a little book, an' when ever'thing was ready Gener'l Forrest, foller'd by five men on foot, rid down the line.

"'Whar is the men that had charge

"'Stan' back from the door, whoever you are!'"

of the jail?' he axed. 'Let 'em step out'n the line!'

"Bushrod Claiborne did n't move, but two men stepped out.

"'Who set fire to the jail?' says he.

"'Not me!' 'Not me!' says the two.

"'Who did you leave gyuardin' the jail?' says he. 'P'int him out to me!'

"They went along the line ontell they got to whar Bushrod Claiborne was standin' pertendin' to laugh an' talk to the man on his left, an' thar they stopped.

"'Show 'im to me!' says the Gener'l; 'put your hand on 'im!'

"An' when they did, Bushrod Claiborne flinched like some un had slapped his face.

"'What is it?' he says to the man. 'Did you speak to me?'

"Then the Gener'l turned to me.

"'Mr. Sanders,' says he, 'who sot the jail a-fire?'

"'Bushrod Claiborne,' says I.

"'Mooneyham!' says the Gener'l, jest as ef he was callin' the roll. 'Mooneyham!' Wi' that Mooneyham come out of the crowd aroun' the Gener'l like a mole out'n the ground. 'Ef you know a man named Bushrod Claiborne, an' he's in that line thar, p'int him out!'

"'Thar he is!' says Mr. Mooneyham.

"The five men that had foller'd Gener'l Forrest along the line was standin' right by his hoss. He jest nodded his head at 'em, an' turned away. This was what they was waitin' for, an' they jest walked to Bushrod Claiborne, ketched holt on him, an' pulled him along wi' 'em. An' then for the fust time he got an idee of what wuz up. He holler'd for the Gener'l.

"'Gener'l Forrest,' he says, 'this is an outrage! Won't you hear what I 've got to say? One word for the sake of ol' times?'

"The Gener'l paid no more attention to him than ef he 'd 'a' been a tom-cat on a back fence a mile away.

"When we rid out'n that town, wi' Forrest an' his men," continued Mr. Sanders, looking as solemn as he could, "Wimberly Driscoll was wi' Margaret an' her mammy. I says to the Gener'l, says I: 'Gener'l, what was done wi' Bushrod Claiborne?'

"'Don't you know?' he says. 'Then come here. A tender-hearted man like you oughter see all that 's to be seed.' Wi' that he pulled his hoss to one side. 'Do you see that black thing a-swingin' in the wind?'

"The Gener'l looked at me hard a minnit an' then he says: 'Mr. Sanders, go home wi' Driscoll an' his friends, an' git in a good big cradle, an' let some nice 'oman rock you to sleep. What you need is rest.'

"I said no more, but for miles an' miles — yes, an' for days an' days — I could feel the shadder of that black, swingin' thing right betwixt my shoulder-blades; an' when I'm off in my feed I can feel it yit; sometimes it's cold, sometimes it's hot."

Mr. Sanders rose, wiped his rosy face with a red handkerchief, and went toddling across the public square.

THE END